ISBN 0-7683-2565-X

Written by Lisa Weedn
Illustrated by Flavia Weedn
© Weedn Family Trust
www.flavia.com
All rights reserved.

Published in 2002 by Cedco Publishing Company
100 Pelican Way, San Rafael, California 94901
For a free catalog of other Cedco® products, please write
to the address above, or visit our website: www.cedco.com

Printed in China

1 3 5 7 9 10 8 6 4 2

If you have comments, suggestions, or just want to share,
we'd love to hear from you. Please write to:
lisa@flaviagirl.com

With love and endless gratitude to
Sylvie, Lisa M., Heather, Amber, Jesse, Jessica, and the Bellini Family.

a healing workbook for girls

holdin' on

a brave girl's guide
to surviving change

Written by Lisa Weedn
Illustrated by Flavia Weedn

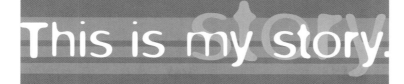
This is my story.

_____

written by

_____

starting date

Table of Contents

TALKIN' ABOUT MY GENERATION

Sometimes it's hard to understand the world we live in. It's hard to understand a lot of things. Life swirls around us so fast, and just as we're busy trying to find our groove, something happens. Something really big. Suddenly, without warning, we feel as if we've been hit. Hard. And it's all we can do to hold on.

At times like these, our thoughts and feelings tend to blur into a hailstorm of grief and sadness, fear, anger, and confusion. Intense emotions rise up. Often they change from one moment to the next. We're baffled. We're in pain. Sometimes we're blinded by the intensity of it all. And we're forced to dig deep within ourselves to summon the strength, compassion, and understanding we need just to get through another day.

Even when bad stuff is happening, there is still good to be found. It's all in how we choose to see, and in which lens we are looking through. But even that's difficult when we're so numb we don't know where to begin to look. Still, there's a way. We always have a choice. And it's important we remember this.

Within each of us there is a source of wisdom and courage that we may not know is there. And yet before we can tap into the lioness's heart within us, we first need to take a good look inside and out, to examine the reality of whatever it is we're facing, and to listen closely—very closely—to what we're feeling inside. Finding our own truth is how we begin to heal. It's how faith and understanding channel their way from our hearts and into our lives.

When we're hurting, or when our peace has been threatened, it's human nature to want to shut down or to cry out. But if we take the time to define our emotions, we come to understand ourselves. When we begin to understand ourselves, we find clarity, purpose, meaning and hope. Even within our pain, we find the strength to carry on.

These pages are yours to befriend. Let them be a key to help you unlock the door to your mind, heart, and spirit. Let them comfort you with your own echo. Let them teach you about things you need to know. Let them hold you gently, bring you courage, and guide you through the storm.

You are the brave.

you are the brave

Just gimme some truth

I think

I feel

I hurt

I hope

I dream

My TRUTH

has many layers,

yet only one inner guide.

I will LISTEN to the

WISDOM of my HEART.

I will gain the COURAGE

to embrace change and

the STRENGTH to carry on.

I will LEARN to not judge

myself for the VERY things

that make ME who I am.

I will find LOVE in

FORGIVENESS,

and GRACE in knowing

that every moment is a GIFT.

I will FIND my way.

We know you've got a lot going on. You're smart and strong and capable. You hold it all together, sometimes you hold it inside, and yet beneath those layers of control there's a tender side of you that thinks and feels deeply. Allowing yourself to feel means you're in touch. It means you're being authentic, you're courageous and you care. It never ever means you're weak. This is key information.

There's a reason you're holding this book. Maybe your heart is breaking, maybe things are out of control, maybe you're frightened, or you're just tired of keeping all those feelings locked up inside. Well, the most important thing for you to remember is that you are not alone. Change touches us all. No matter how big or small, change can bring sadness and uncertainty. It can shake your foundation and turn your world upside down. Yet it can also show you the true strength you are made of. Feeling your way through the hard times is part of the journey called life.

Adversity—whether you're dealing with the fear of war, the pain of losing a loved one, the divorce of your parents, the breakup of a relationship, an illness, a move, a change of schools, or any other heartache that has you feeling like you're in the middle of a powerful storm—can rock you so deeply that you think your world won't survive. But wait. Hold on. The fact that you're reading this says a lot about you. It says that you recognize the light of hope that is already within you. To confront the fear and to consciously find your way out of the dark means you're willing to grow. To seek understanding means you've made the choice not to stay stuck in the hurt or the panic. And within every challenge you endure in life, there are always hidden gifts just waiting to be discovered. (Trust us on this one.)

Okay then, so how do you tap into that wise and brilliantly brave psyche of yours? By taking the first step. Start by describing the landscape, the history, the scene. Whatever's going on around you, who did what to whom, or what caused you to find yourself right here, right now. Everyone's got a story to tell. And every story has to begin somewhere. So what's yours? What happened? What's the deal?

You're safe here, so just grab your pen and let it spill.

What's Going On?

the beginning

It all started when…

the serious stuff

And then…

{ I have hope. I have faith.
I am strong, and I am afraid.
But I am not alone. }

Here's an exercise that will help you channel all that angst into art. Make a photo essay, a paper mosaic, a drawing, or a collage that visually describes your world, your heart, whatever is goin' on. Be bold. Unleash the dragon. Use magazine clippings, newspaper headlines, personal photos, song lyrics, private sketches—anything that tells your story.

what am I feeling

Emotions can be silent and invisible or loud and obvious. They can hit so hard that they send you crashing to the ground or screaming out in a rage, or they can leave you stunned, motionless, and frozen in disbelief. They can make you feel so exhausted from thinking about them that you just want to tune out, but hard as you try that voice keeps coming at you—in song lyrics, in dreams, in the faces of the people you love.

What can you do?

Well, whatever has happened in your life, this is the time to really listen to your thoughts. Yep, even though it might seem like you can't deal with them anymore, this is exactly when you need to take ownership of your feelings, put a name to your emotions, and allow yourself the opportunity to compassionately examine the inner workings of your soul. Why? Because stuffing them inside or denying them will only cause their power over you to intensify. So gather up your strength, accept whatever it is you're feeling, and do a face-off. Look directly at those emotional dragons and talk right at 'em. By the time you're finished, you'll be amazed at how much power you've taken back (and those dragons won't have a chance).

Ready? Set? Cool. Now go.

sadness

What hurts?

{ Feelings are never right or wrong. To feel is to prove I exist. }

Fear

What am I most afraid of?

_____
_____
_____
_____
_____
_____
_____
_____
_____
_____
_____
_____
_____
_____
_____
_____
_____
_____
_____
_____
_____
_____
_____

{ Sometimes I must face the fear before I can pass through it. }

{ Change, even when it hurts,
can be a catalyst to miraculous growth. }

What is with this fire inside of me?

Anger

> { Life is a journey filled with lessons, and each one makes me stronger. }

Do I feel stuck? Am I sinking in quicksand or just frozen in time?

helplessness

guilt

What's with the guilt trip? Is there really anything I could have done to prevent this from happening?

_____
_____
_____
_____
_____
_____
_____
_____
_____
_____
_____
_____
_____
_____
_____
_____
_____
_____
_____
_____
_____
_____
_____
_____
_____
_____
_____
_____
_____
_____
_____

{ Blame is a path that leads me nowhere. Forgiveness is a higher journey, filled with light and wisdom and untapped strength. }

cause and effect

Identifying your feelings is a major accomplishment. Good for you, girl! That's courage. That's like peeling back the toughest layer. And now comes the real learning. (Don't even think of stopping now!)

Take a minute to look over what you've already written. You'll probably be surprised by some of the things you wrote. That's good. That's discovery. Now think about how your emotions have affected you. You know, that unavoidable reaction to every action, like: "when I think about what hurts I can't stop crying (or the tears just won't come)," or "there's this constant ball of fear in me and suddenly I'm staring at the TV screen for hours (or refusing to turn it on at all)," or "I'm so worried that all I do is eat or wonder why I feel so numb, or why I can't concentrate on my schoolwork, or why I just want to lock myself up in my room." You get the picture.

The way we act and the things we choose to do are a reflection of how we're feeling inside. If you're feeling crummy, it's gonna show. If you're feeling like things are way out of control, you may be acting way out of control. That's when you can really get into trouble. Like doing risky stuff that can only hurt you more in the long run. Don't go there. Take back control of your life. Make a point to really look at how you're behaving, what you're doing to ease the pain, if you're running from it or trying to mask it or if you're really working hard to face it. This stuff is really important because it's a good bet that you're probably unaware of some of your behaviors. And hey, awareness is fundamental. So c'mon. Give it a try. Look deeper.

How am I relating (or not) to others? Am I suddenly a social magnet, taking cover in the company of a ton of friends? Or have I become a loner, not wanting to be around anyone? Has my schoolwork suffered? How have I let events affect my personal relationships?

How's my attitude? What am I showing on the outside? Am I loud? Quiet? Moody? Extra nice or short-tempered? Kind or unkind? Do I store it all up, then fall apart over the little things? Did I used to be a more positive, upbeat person? Am I silently sulking, or am I just numb?

mood swings and outbursts

What are my forms of release? Am I active? Inactive? Am I laughing nervously at everything because I'm afraid that if I don't then I might start crying and never stop? Do I show my emotions in front of others, or do I save them for when I'm all alone? Do I roar or do I whine? Do I exercise or play music or write poetry or dive into my schoolwork or tell my story over and over again to anyone who will listen? How do I let off the steam?

_____
_____
_____
_____
_____
_____
_____
_____
_____
_____
_____
_____
_____
_____
_____
_____
_____
_____

{ It takes real courage to look in the mirror and see myself for who I am, but I must know myself before the world can know me. }

eatinghabits

Am I easing the pain with a pint of ice cream and a bag of chips all in one sitting (and still hungry for more)? Or am I on a hunger strike, trying to starve my emotions by starving myself? How do I deal with food? Is it comfort or nourishment? What's healthy about my relationship with food and what's not?

{ Running away from the pain or masking the hurt only delays my progress. I will stay aware and seek a healthy balance. }

{ I have permission to be who I am, and to feel what I feel. }
It's okay to be gentle with myself.

How am I treating myself? Am I kind to me or do I beat myself up? Do I let myself smile? What am I doing that is good for me? What am I doing that is not so good for me? How do I nurture my spirit?

What role does my faith play in all of this? Do I take the time to pray or meditate? What spiritual comfort do I reach for? How do my beliefs fit into this picture?

_____
_____
_____
_____
_____
_____
_____
_____
_____
_____
_____
_____
_____
_____
_____
_____
_____
_____
_____
_____
_____
_____
_____
_____

{ Faith is the hand I hold in times of light or shadow. }

Who am I letting in? Who do I look to for guidance? Who do I lean on? Who do I trust?

_____
_____
_____
_____
_____
_____
_____
_____
_____
_____
_____
_____
_____
_____
_____
_____
_____
_____
_____
_____
_____
_____
_____
_____

friends and family

Poetry can be an elixir, a healing force, a release like no other. You don't have to be an accomplished writer to spill beauty from your pen. The only requirement is to feel. And baby, you've got that one down, so give this exercise a try.

Think of one word that describes your life or how you're feeling at this very moment. Then run with it. If your emotions were an animal, what breed would they be? If love had a color, if fear had a sound, if hope had a texture, what would it look like, sound like, feel like? Look around your room, find one treasure that brings you comfort or stirs up a ton of emotion. Write about it. Or think of a person who has touched your soul like no other. Tell them how you feel and say all those words you could never say out loud. Let yourself be inspired in ways you never thought of before.

There aren't any rules here. Just release all that pent up stuff and let it flow. (Hey, no one ever has to read it unless you want 'em to!) You can be light, reflective, and loving, or dark and edgy. You can be silly or insightful. You don't have to rhyme (in fact, it's better if you don't). This is freestyle cleansing. This is beauty unleashed. This is about pain or chaos or tenderness finding it's way out of your heart and transforming itself into art. Let go. Let it happen. Set your spirit free.

poetry

You're on an awesome roll! You're making real progress and showing yourself the capacity of your heart. Can you feel it? Cool. We're proud of you, and you should be, too!

Now you can take a well-deserved break. Stretch, listen to a favorite CD, take a walk, hug your cat, smile, laugh, and let yourself lighten up. (Give yourself permission, it's okay!) Then as soon as you're ready, come back to this section and dig in a little deeper.

You've identified your emotions, you've learned how they're affecting your behavior, you've even written poetry to soothe your soul. Now it's time to take all this new knowledge and channel it into positive energy. This is where the healing happens.

Ask yourself what you really want. What's important to you? What do you value? What do you dream of? What do you seek? And why? Then just start writing and don't quit until you run out of words.
(Yeah right, like that's ever gonna happen!)

Let go of the little stuff and concentrate on the big picture. What really matters most to you?

what is most important to me?

{ Every person on earth has the right to be free, to be loved, and to reach for a dream. }

Imagine. If the world could be of your design, what would life be like?

_____
_____
_____
_____
_____
_____
_____
_____
_____
_____
_____
_____
_____
_____
_____
_____
_____
_____
_____
_____
_____
_____
_____
_____
_____
_____

what would change if I could?

changechangechange

You're more powerful than you might think. Every dream begins with you, and nothing is impossible to a believing heart. So keep talkin' and stir it up. Change begins with you.

{ We are unaware of what sweet miracles may come. }

What's love got to do with it? Everything! All that you feel inside has love at its core. Whether it's romantic love, family love, or love for mankind, speak up! Write about what role love plays in your life and what it means to you.

_____
_____
_____
_____
_____
_____
_____
_____
_____
_____
_____
_____
_____
_____
_____
_____
_____
_____
_____
_____
_____
_____
_____
_____
_____

{ To love and to be loved is life's greatest reward.
Love is everything. Love is all that matters. }

> We are all connected in this life
> and the act of caring is about building foundations of
> trust, love, respect, compassion, and understanding.

Compassion, understanding and forgiveness are at the root of all spiritual and personal growth. They are conscious decisions we make to accept that we're all human, and to practice tolerance as we release all that blame. Open that beautiful heart, expand your mind, and take the high road. How do you use these precious tools in relation to others? And hey, don't forget this one: How compassionate and forgiving are you with yourself?

thoughts on compassion forgiveness & understanding

{ I believe in freedom and human rights and fair treatment to all living things. I believe in taking a stand. }

You've already written a little about what role your faith plays in your life. Here is where you can be more specific about what you believe in or don't. What are your values? What do you consider morally right and what are the things you are absolutely against? Take a stand, girl, and speak your mind.

_____
_____
_____
_____
_____
_____
_____
_____
_____
_____
_____
_____
_____
_____
_____
_____
_____
_____
_____
_____
_____
_____
_____
_____

thoughts or beliefs & moral values

thoughts on peace & freedom

Big topics, huh? You bet. Share your thoughts on a peaceful world, a peaceful heart, a free country, or the freedom to think and do as you please in the privacy of your own space. Take a global look, take an inner view, then bring it on home. Talk about what peace and freedom mean to you and your life.

_____
_____
_____
_____
_____
_____
_____
_____
_____
_____
_____
_____
_____
_____
_____
_____
_____
_____
_____
_____
_____

{ I believe there are miracles happening
even when I can't see them. }

thoughts on the future

What are your thoughts on the future? No doom and gloom allowed, just visualize the best possible outcome. Positivity is key. What do you wish for yourself, for your family, for your country, for our world? What do you desire? Where do you want to go, what do you want to experience in your life? Hey, it all starts with a vision and every reality is born of a dream. Remember, only you can decide your future; the power is all yours.

{ I believe that my life has purpose and that I was put here to make a difference. }

{ Hope is the song inside my heart that will never stop singing. }

Somewhere amid the hurt and the angst and the tough realizations you've been exploring, you've likely seen a glimmer of hope reveal itself. Well, grab a hold of that hope, put it in your pocket and seize its power. Use it. Polish it. Put it down on paper so you never forget it's there.   What brings me hope? What makes me feel good about myself and my life? What dreams do I hold close? What motivates me?

pockets of hope

Remember when you were a little girl
and you just learned to ride a bike? Or skate? Or
dance? Or ride a scooter? Remember how hard it was to find
your balance? Remember when you fell and skinned your knee and you
were way embarrassed in front of that cute neighbor boy? Okay, so the trick was
to just get back to it and to keep trying over and over until you felt the wind in your
face and your confidence soared, right? Same thing goes here. Any time you fall in life,
the best thing to do is to get up, brush yourself off, straighten your sassy little skirt, and keep
on going. Keep on trying. Keep on believing. Don't ever give up.

Getting back in the groove and reestablishing your normal routines is a good thing. So is adding a
few new rituals, too. We're talkin' healthy stuff. Stuff that keeps you grounded and helps you
remember who you are (like a new exercise program, time for meditation or prayer or yoga, taking
up a new musical instrument, a new art form, a weekly hike or swim, or just about anything that
brings you joy and added clarity).

Begin by designing your ideal day, then include the things you know you have to do
(school, chores, job, whatever). Make a schedule and follow it for a week. Write it in
pencil. If it doesn't feel good, erase it and start over. Keep it up 'til it feels right.
Just get back into your life, feel good about knowing that you're wiser
than you were before, reclaim your groove, and let the wind
carry you.

monday

7 am	3 pm
8 am	4 pm
9 am	5 pm
10 am	6 pm
11 am	7 pm
12 pm	8 pm
1 pm	9 pm
2 pm	10 pm

Tuesday

7 am	3 pm
8 am	4 pm
9 am	5 pm
10 am	6 pm
11 am	7 pm
12 pm	8 pm
1 pm	9 pm
2 pm	10 pm

wednesday

7 am	3 pm
8 am	4 pm
9 am	5 pm
10 am	6 pm
11 am	7 pm
12 pm	8 pm
1 pm	9 pm
2 pm	10 pm

thursday

7 am	3 pm
8 am	4 pm
9 am	5 pm
10 am	6 pm
11 am	7 pm
12 pm	8 pm
1 pm	9 pm
2 pm	10 pm

friday

7 am	3 pm
8 am	4 pm
9 am	5 pm
10 am	6 pm
11 am	7 pm
12 pm	8 pm
1 pm	9 pm
2 pm	10 pm

saturday

7 am	3 pm
8 am	4 pm
9 am	5 pm
10 am	6 pm
11 am	7 pm
12 pm	8 pm
1 pm	9 pm
2 pm	10 pm

7 am	3 pm
8 am	4 pm
9 am	5 pm
10 am	6 pm
11 am	7 pm
12 pm	8 pm
1 pm	9 pm
2 pm	10 pm

Talkin' about my generation

I learn

I act

I help

heal

I love

This world I live in

is a complicated place.

It is filled with BEAUTY and injustice,

with LOVE and with sadness.

But I know who I am

and I BELIEVE in me.

I will find my way

with the POWER of my mind

and the TRUTH of my heart.

I will embrace

the FREEDOM to speak out

on what I believe in.

I will surround myself

with those I love and RESPECT.

I will dare to LIVE the life I DREAM.

reality check

The coolest thing about living in a world with so many people in it is that there are plenty of others just like you who are going through similar stuff. They may or may not live next door, but they're out there just the same. Some of them are authors or artists or musicians or athletes. Some are famous and some are just average teens feeling the same things that you do. Wouldn't it be cool to find them? Well, here's your chance. All it takes is a bit of research.

Start by coming up with a few key words. Pick the topics closest to your heart and begin searching the internet, the library, the bookstore. Look for sites that address your concerns. Find articles, columns, or advice commentaries that speak the language of your heart. Talk to your friends, your teachers, your parents, your siblings, your counselor at school, or anyone you trust for tips on what to read or where to go. Check out youth groups or organizations, charities or local chapters that address stuff that really interests you. Read magazines and take note of who wrote the pieces you especially liked. Do the same with newspapers and song lyrics. Become a fact-finding fanatic, a research maniac. Open your mind. Listen. Absorb. Keep notes. Seek your psychological soul mates. So many people are talking and it's healing to hear what they have to say.

Knowing that another person actually "gets it" can feel like a bright light coming on in a dark room. Suddenly you aren't alone anymore and you can see things in a whole new perspective. Remember, isolation is only a state of mind. Change the mindset, girl, and everything changes—for the better. Promise.

My Topics

My Keywords

insightful wisdom

Helpful Websites and Links

Cool Chats, Newsgroups, Forums

{ I am not ashamed to reach out and ask for help. }

My Notes

Brilliant Books and Authors, Magazines, Commentaries, Newsletters

Awesome Music, Lyricists, Bands

{ We are each a part of one another
and connected by the grand dance we call life. }

My Notes

{ Sometimes when I look at life
through someone else's drama,
my own life becomes richer. }

61

Inspiring Lectures, Gatherings, Activities, or Classes to Attend

Supportive Clubs, Groups, or Organizations

{ Communication is the key that unlocks the door to healing. }

My life has been made richer by
simple acts of kindness, expressions of confidence,
and someone else's way of speaking a truth that finally made sense.

My Notes

comfort zone

Best People to Hang With

Favorite Places to Be

{ Real friends share laughter, love, and tears.
They understand the meaning between the words. }

My Notes

{ Real friends never criticize or lead me to
do things that are unhealthy for my mind, body, and spirit. }

Learning to Listen

Stuff I'm learning about myself and others, stuff I'm learning about life...

{ Life is brief and very fragile;
there is little time to leave words unsaid. }

Words I still need to say out loud (and to whom)...

Taming the Dragon

What important truths do you wish you could share with others who are going through what you've gone through? What pains of yours have been eased, and how? What knowledge have you gained and how has it helped you to become a better person?

{ Beyond the mask, beneath the armor,
the essence of me is waiting for a chance to be heard. }

Letting Go

Sometimes we have to let go of some things in order to hold on to what's really important. Know what we mean? Like saying goodbye to toxic relationships (so you can make room for healthy ones); like abandoning the fear of your parents remarrying (and giving happiness a chance); or like letting yourself hold on to the belief that good stuff can and will happen (even when bad stuff is going on). Good. So what are you learning to let go of? What no longer serves you? What are you choosing to keep? Take some time on this one. It'll be worth it.

{ I believe in the power of love.
It helps me to understand what really matters
and to let go of the things that don't. }

After enduring hardship, or even while in the midst of it, if you step outside of your own drama long enough to see the bigger picture and how connected we all are to one another, your heart expands and so does your view of life. Giving to others is one of the best ways to heal. So whether you can help a little or a lot, reach out. There's no better therapy.

Life is never a solo journey. *{When I give from the heart, I receive in return.}*

Charities, Organizations, Groups

Places I Can Help

sharing the light

taking Action

List five things I can do or ways I can help right now.

1 _____
_____
_____

2 _____
_____
_____

3 _____
_____
_____

4 _____
_____
_____

5 _____
_____
_____

{ My actions speak louder than my words.
When I take the time to give to others,
my path in life becomes clearer. }

Positive Perspective

It's all about perspective. List five great things that still rock about my life.

1

2

3

4

5

{ The landscape of my world is bigger than I can see.
Beyond the horizon, life awaits my touch. }

Taking Care of Me

Make a commitment. List five things that I promise to do for myself that will keep me grounded, positive, healthy, hopeful, and sane.

1

2

3

4

5

{ When I take the time to care for me, negativity melts away and the world can see me for who I really am. }

theGoodStuff

Remember at the beginning of this book when you made a visual collage of your life and everything that led you here? Well, now you get to make one that shows all the good stuff. Include bits of wisdom you've gained, things you've learned, stuff you almost forgot to remember until now. Use magazine clippings, newspaper headlines, personal photos, song lyrics, private sketches—look through a new lens and retell your story.

discovering the Gift

Major changes in life can't help but shape the person you are and the person you will become; they will always be a part of you. And because you've allowed yourself to fully experience your thoughts, feelings, and emotions, you have grown more aware, built your character, strengthened your resolve, witnessed the capacity of your believing heart, and become a more enlightened and understanding person.

You've just learned that even in the face of pain, there is always love. And learning to love yourself and others can be one powerful awakening. In spite of the fear, you've found a way to cope; in spite of uncertainty, you have found faith enough to hold on, to look at things in a new light, to embrace the good and to share it with others.

In going through this process, we hope you've come to find the hidden gifts that you were meant to discover. They're unique and different for everyone, so make sure you write them down now while the glow is still fresh. Within them you'll find the keys that will always be with you. You can use them anytime you need them to unlock your heart and to help you remember what is most important. Please protect the gifts you've found. They're precious and irreplaceable. And so are you.

you are precious

protecting the Gift

What truths have I discovered? What are the hidden gifts I have found? What private sanctuary or safe place (in my mind if not literally) will I create that will help me remember the power of my heart? How will I tap into love? How will I keep hope alive forever?

Reflection & Insight

Revisit this book from time to time and write about your progress. Add your personal insights, your memories, your wisdom. Keep a log of your learning, things you are thankful for, the poetry, lines, and lyrics that you love, the people and things that help you get through each day. Hold on to the faith. Continue to embrace the gift. Always remember. Never forget.

Through thankfulness, I can learn the wisdom of the ages. I only need to look within to hear the voice of love.

Remembrance & Gratitude

{ Love is the sharing of songs and of silences,
and the holding of memories only the heart can see.
Remember everything. }